Antique Toothbrush Holders

John, Nancy & Brooke Smith

Schiffer Publishing Ltd

4880 Lower Valley Road, Atglen, PA 19310 USA

Dedication

To our son and brother Todd,
an avid supporter and fellow collector.

Type set in Dutch 801 Rm BT
Designed by Kevin Kelly
Cover by Bruce Waters

ISBN: 0-7643-1654-0
Printed in China
1 2 3 4

Published by Schiffer Publishing Ltd.
4880 Lower Valley Road
Atglen, PA 19310
Phone: (610) 593-1777; Fax: (610) 593-2002
E-mail: Schifferbk@aol.com
Please visit our web site catalog at **www.schifferbooks.com**
We are always looking for people to write books on new and
related subjects. If you have an idea for a book please
contact us at the above address.

This book may be purchased from the publisher.
Include $3.95 for shipping.
Please try your bookstore first.
You may write for a free catalog.

In Europe, Schiffer books are distributed by
Bushwood Books
6 Marksbury Ave.
Kew Gardens
Surrey TW9 4JF England
Phone: 44 (0) 20 8392-8585; Fax: 44 (0) 20 8392-9876
E-mail: Bushwd@aol.com
Free postage in the U.K., Europe; air mail at cost.

Contents

Introduction

The earliest toothbrush holders known date from the first half of the nineteenth century. Usually made of a ceramic or ironstone material, they were simple in design and are identifiable as toothbrush holders only from old catalog descriptions.

In 1898 a pressed glass toothbrush holder was advertised by the U.S. Glass Company. It was clearly meant for toothbrushes. Designed to be hung on the wall, the design was two toothbrushes held by a bow. Through the loops in the bow two "real wax back brushes pass, handle downward, and the bristles upward and outward. The holder makes a handsome wall ornament, being made in plain crystal, gold decorated, emerald and emerald in gold decoration." The same design was used for the cup-like holder shown here, though the loops of the bow are closed.

The advertisement for the holder concluded:

> "A clean tooth behind ruby lips is pleasant to the eye, and the importance of regularly using a tooth brush, and therefore demonstrating the necessity of having the utensils handy, is very strongly brought out in a recent journal devoted to dentistry, and which might have been very properly pressed into the tooth brush holder. Thus: 'A clean tooth will not decay in a hundred years.'"

Green pressed glass holder. United States Glass Co., circa 1898. United States. 4-3/4". $295-350.

The importance of clean teeth was not lost on parents who engaged in the perennial struggle of getting their children to brush. The figural toothbrush holders which began to appear in the 1920s were designed to help in their challenge. Using whimsical characters, animals, nursery rhymes, sports, occupations, deco animals and figures, holidays, and, later, cartoon characters, hundreds of toothbrush holders were created to encourage children to brush more frequently.

The heyday of the figural toothbrush holder was the 1920s and the 1930s, though they continued to be popular in the 1950s and are still being manufactured and enjoyed today. With all the thousands of holders that have been made over the years, one would think that the antique marketplace would be flooded with examples. Three things must be remembered, however. First, that toothbrush holders were usually made of fragile ceramic materials, second, they were kept in tiled bathrooms, and, third, they were used primarily by children. It seems that a large majority of the holders found a tragic end on a cold hard floor.

Toothbrush holders were made in a variety of materials. The earliest were ironstone, porcelain, bisque, or other ceramics. Over the years they were made in glass, chalkware, celluloid, plastic, and lithographed tin.

The body of this figure is a container for tooth powder.

Flow blue "Blossom" pattern, circa 1865. The toothbrush holder is attached to a tray in this one-piece construction. 6-1/2". $350-450.

In the earliest bisque figural holders, the body of the piece was designed as a shaker for tooth powder, usually made with a place to hold the toothbrush. As tooth powder went out of fashion and toothpaste came into use, the holders changed their form. Often the figures were meant only for toothbrushes, sometimes being designed with a hole that would hold the brush in a strategic position, like the tail of horse, golf clubs, a fiddle neck, or a witch's broom. In other cases, the figure concealed or complemented the place that held the toothbrushes.

A clever design using the toothbrush as the witch's broom.

Many holders also had a place for toothpaste. Since at that time toothpaste tubes were much smaller than today, they sometimes sat on a tray at the base of the holder. In other cases a place for the tube was incorporated into the overall design. Occasionally, the toothbrush holder would include a place for a cup or soap in addition to the toothpaste.

The manufacturers of Dr. West's Tooth Paste sold this rabbit toothbrush holder with a convenient tray...just the right size for a tube of Dr. West's.

Toothbrush holders took several forms. The most popular were freestanding, some of which could also hang on the wall. Occasionally, the freestanding holders were designed to fit into corners. Other toothbrush holders were designed only to be mounted on the wall.

There are several areas of debate among collectors of toothbrush holders. While none of them can be settled here, they are worthy of note. Some collectors will only buy holders that have trays for toothpaste, believing that this is the only true way to determine if the figure was actually intended for toothbrushes. Among the holders illustrated here you will find many that have no tray but are clearly made to hold toothbrushes. As you will see, probably less than half have a toothpaste tray or holder.

Other collectors will only buy toothbrush holders that have rectangular holes. While this is true of a slight majority of holders, it far from a determining factor. Indeed many holders with toothpaste trays have square, oval, or round holes. Sometimes the round hole is consistent with the overall design of the piece, and sometimes it is just the designer's choice. In either case, it is not the determining factor.

Finally, there are many collectors who believe a toothbrush holder must have a drain hole in the base. Again, too many obvious toothbrush holders have no hole for this to be a firm rule.

That being said, the truth is that sometimes it is hard to tell a toothbrush holder from a vase or other novelty. The three factors named above should be considered, but the collector needs to add a dose of common sense and experience.

Most antique toothbrush holders were made in Germany or Japan. Those from Germany are more highly valued than the Japanese. They were superior in design, paint, and glazing, usually showing much more detail and imagination. The Japanese holders were often based on other's designs, and the workmanship was not up to the German standards. Some of the Japanese holders were exported exclusively to Australia, never making it to the American market, thus they are rarer and more desirable to today's collector. German holders usually came to the U.S. via English exporters. An exception to this are those imported by the Norwood Co., of Cincinnati, Ohio. They imported directly from Germany, where many of their holders were manufactured by Goebel.

In the United States two manufacturers of toothbrush holders were Miller Studios of North Philadelphia, Ohio, and Cleminson of California.

While all toothbrush holders are becoming harder to find, some are particularly rare or have great appeal to collectors. The miniature holders, under three-inches, seemed to be more prone to breakage because of their size, and are particularly hard to find. Similarly, bisque, due to its fragile nature, is rare in crisp or near-mint condition. Though ethnic forms were popular in other novelty ceramics, there are very few black toothbrush holders, thus increasing their value. As always, early Disney forms command much attention and high prices. This is particularly true of the Pinnochio and Gepetto, Snow White, and the Tortoise and the Hare. Finally, artist-signed pieces are more highly prized, especially those from the Mabel Lucie Attwell series.

The prices given in this book are in ranges. Several factors can influence price. The most important, of course, is condition. Prices also vary by geography, differing from west coast to east coast, and country to country. As always your best source for information is a reputable dealer.

Though no one knows for sure, there are probably over 1500 different designs of toothbrush holders. Each one is unique and most are sure to bring a smile to your face. With such a large variety, everyone can find one that will appeal to their taste and pocketbook. So we hope you enjoy the toothbrush holders pictured here and that they will urge you onward in your own collecting!

People

Boy sitting and playing accordion. Goebel, Germany. 4". $175-225.

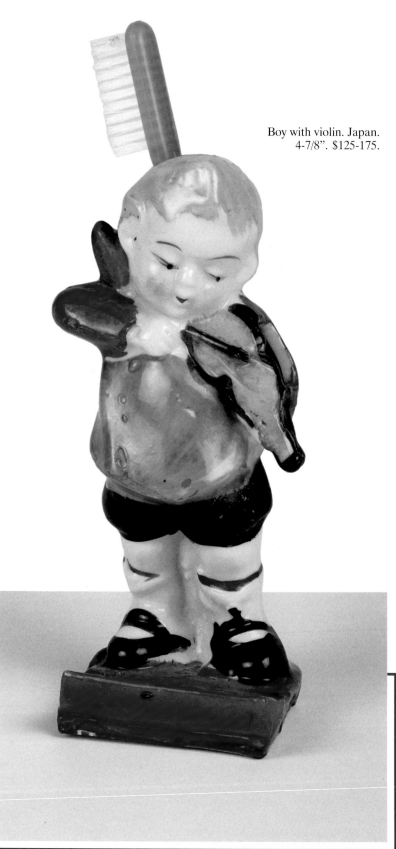

Boy with violin. Japan. 4-7/8". $125-175.

Boy playing flute.
Japan. 4-1/4".
$125-175.

Violinist with Scottie. Goldcastle, Japan. 5". $125-175.

Boy playing cello.
Lustreware,
Japan. 4-1/4".
$125-175.

Clown holding mask. Goldcastle, Japan. 5-1/2". $150-195.

Clown holding hoop. Germany. 4-1/4". $175-225.

Clown holding two balls. Germany. 5-3.4". $275-350.

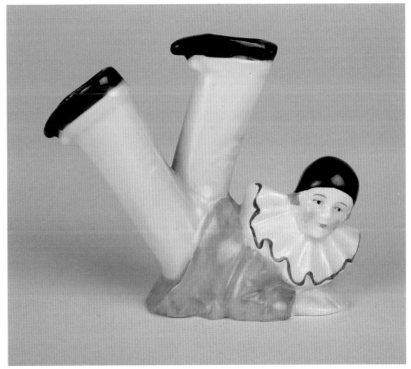

Harlequin with feet up. Germany. 3-1/2". $275-350.

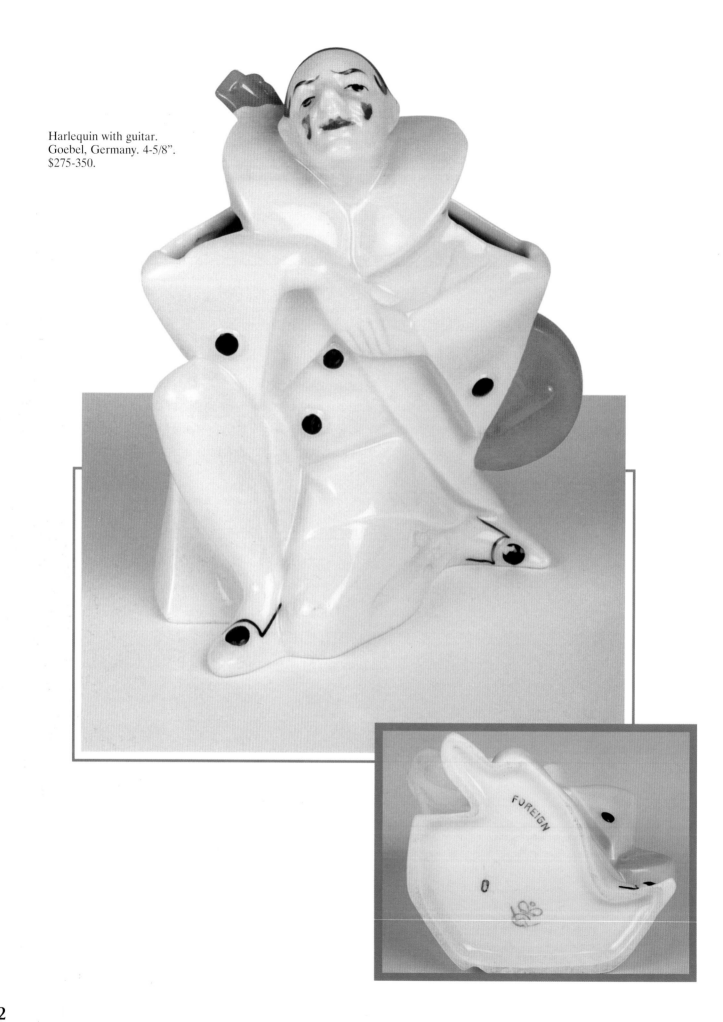

Harlequin with guitar.
Goebel, Germany. 4-5/8".
$275-350.

Clown doing the splits, wall hanging. Germany. 2-3/8". $350-450.

Clown, lustreware. This piece also hangs. Japan. 6-1/2". $125-175.

Clown with horn. Japan. 3-5/8". $50-75.

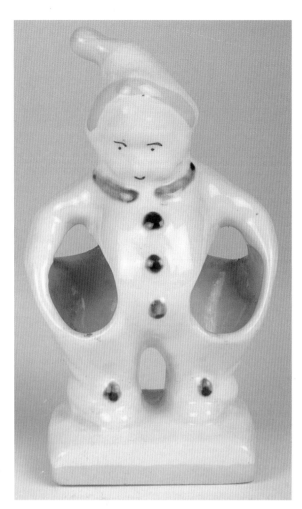

Clown with oversized pockets.
Japan. 5-3/4". $150-195.

Clown with hoop, lustreware. Japan. 6". $175-225.

Clown juggling. Japan.
4-7/8". $125-175.

Clown with hands on hips,
lustreware. Japan. 5-1/2". $175-225.

Clown with hands behind back. Trico, Japan. 6-3/4". $150-195.

Clown with mandolin,
lustreware. Japan. 6". $175-225.

Clown. Germany. 4-1/2". $225-250.   Clown. Japan. 4-7/8". $125-175.

Boy dressed as
clown. Germany.
4-1/4". $250-295.

Standing harlequin. Germany. 5-3/8". $350-450.

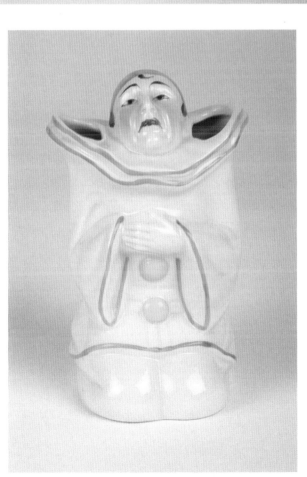

Harlequin kneeling. Germany.
4-1/4". $250-295.

Cowboy, arms crossed.
Japan. 5". $125-175.

Sitting harlequin with bouquet. Germany. 3-5/8". $350-450.

Harlequin sitting
holding bouquet.
Germany. 4-5/8".
$275-350.

Troubadour. Germany. 5-1/2". $250-295.

Cowboy with short brim
hat, lustreware wall. Japan.
6-1/4". $195-225.

Cowboy with wide brim hat, lustreware wall. Japan. 6-1/2". $195-225.

Annie Oakley. Japan. 5-7/8". $195-225.

Cowboy with original toothbrush and Ipana toothpaste. 5-1/8". $150-195.

Soccer player, "Poetst je tanden." Germany. 4". $175-225.

Child holding soccer ball. Germany. 3-1/2". $125-175.

Soccer player. Germany. 3-1/2". $125-175.

Left: skater; right: skier.
Germany. 3-1/8".
$125-175 each.

Golf caddie, bag on right. Japan. 4-1/2". $150-195.

Golf caddie, bag on left. Japan. 4-1/4". $150-195.

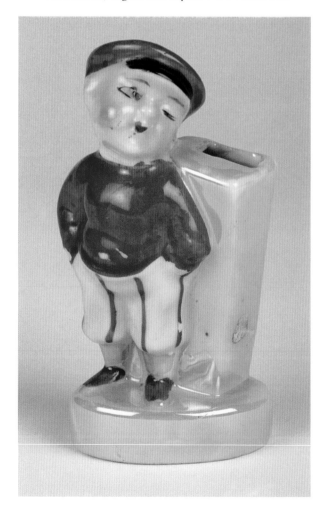

Golf caddie with over-sized bag. Japan. 4-5/8". $150-195.

Golf caddie. Germany. 4-3/8". $325-375.

Caddie boy sitting. Germany. 3-3/8". $150-195.

Girl dressed in riding attire. Germany. 4-1/8". $250-295.

Golfer with club and ball. Germany. 4-3/4". $150-195.

Boy with book. Japan. 5-3/8". $125-175.

24

Boy holding ball. Japan.
5-3/8". $150-195.

Boy with puppy. Japan. 5-1/8". $150-195.

Boy with hands in his pocket.
Japan. 5-1/2". $150-195.

Boy train conductor. Japan. 5-5/8". $150-195.

Boy in lederhosen, shown with
original toothpaste. Goebel,
Germany. 5-1/8". $275-350.

Boy with sash. Japan.
6". $150-195.

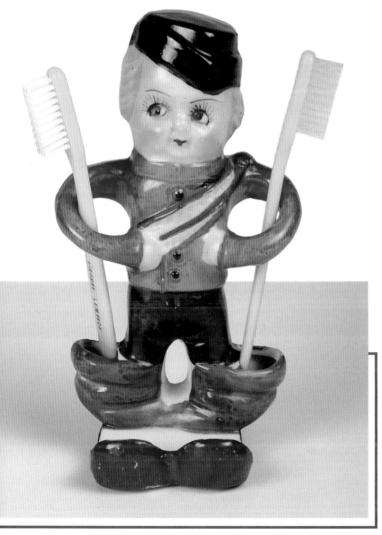

Boy brushing teeth, "toothbrush holder."
Japan. 4-7/8". $150-195.

TOOTHBRUSH
HOLDER

Chimney sweep. Goebel,
Germany. 4-7/8". $325-375.

Boy going to market. Germany. 3-1/2". $125-175.

Boy in oversized boots. Japan. 5-1/8". $150-195.

Boy going to market with two pigs. Japan. 5-1/2". $195-250.

Boy with dog. Japan. 6-3/8". $175-225.

Baby with teddy bear. Germany. 4-1/4". $250-295.

Boy riding elephant. Japan. 6". $150-195.

Boy with bouquet
and wine basket.
Japan. 4-3/8".
$100-150.

Boy with hand in pockets, "Zahncreme Mouson." D.R.G.M.
4-1/8". $250-295.

Cobbler with two
boots. Germany.
4". $175-225.

Colonial man.
Germany. 4-1/4".
$250-295.

Boy with hand in pockets, bisque. Germany.
6-3/4". $350-450.

Man in top hat
and tails, also a
powder shaker.
Germany. 4-1/4".
$275-350.

Whimsical man with cane and bouquet of flowers, lustreware. Germany. 3-3/4". $275-350.

Boy with bouquet of flowers, bisque. Germany. 4-7/8". $175-225.

Boy sitting. Combination toothbrush holder and soap dish; may be hung on wall. "Wasch je handen, poets je tanden." Holland. 4-1/2". $275-350.

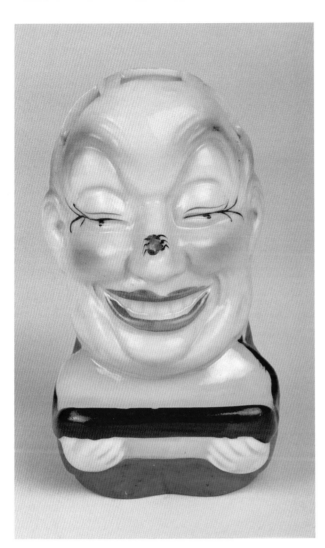

Whimsical man with fly on
nose. Japan. 4-7/8". $175-225.

Boy with basket, lustreware
hanger. Japan. 3-5/8".
$125-175.

Boy brushing dogs teeth, "A
present from Barry Island."
Germany. 3-5/8". $150-195.

English bobby. Japan. 5-7/8". $175-225.

English bobby. Germany. 5". $295-325.

Police boy. Germany.
4-1/2". $225-250.

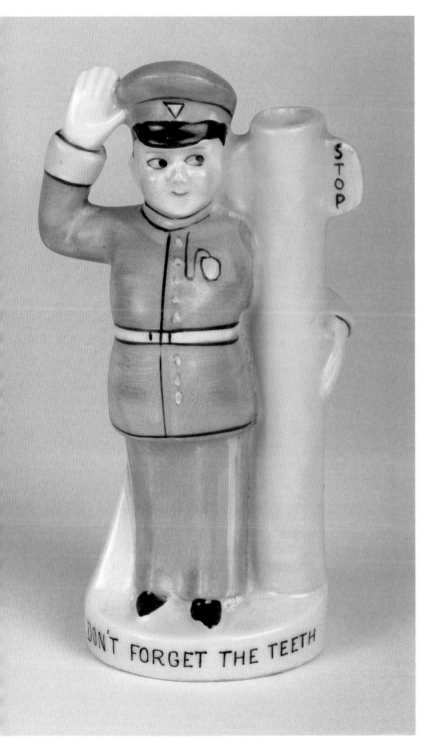

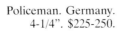

Policeman by stop sign, "Don't forget the teeth." Germany.
5-1/2". $250-295.

Policeman. Germany.
4-1/4". $225-250.

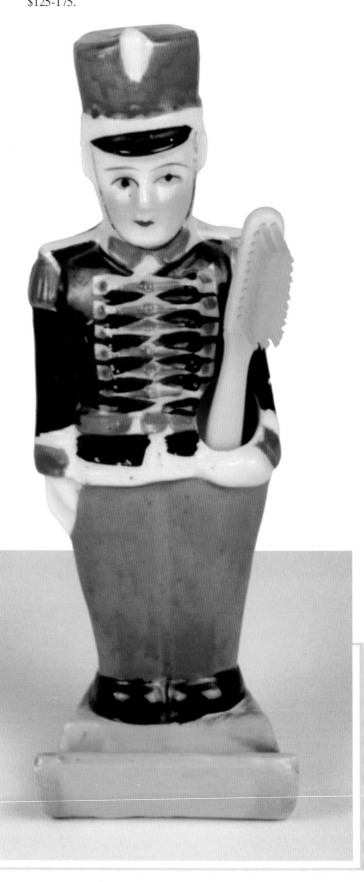

Soldier. Japan. 6-1/2".
$125-175.

Toy soldier, missing cup. "G.W. Co., Germany." 4-1/2". $275-350.

Bellhop with luggage.
Bavaria. 6-5/8".
$295-325.

Bellhop by mailbox. Germany. 4". $250-295.

Bellhop with luggage.
Germany. 4-3/8".
$250-295.

Bellhop, lustreware.
This piece also hangs.
Trico, Japan. 6-1/2".
$150-195.

Train conductor. Japan. 5-1/8". $150-195.

Bellhop. Germany. 5-1/4".
$175-225.

Drum major, plastic. Hong Kong. 7". $50-100.

Drum major. Superior, Japan. 6-1/4". $150-225.

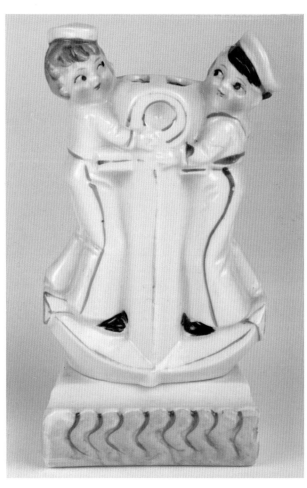

Sailor boy and girl on anchor. Japan. 5-1/2". $150-195.

Sailor boy, lustreware. Japan. 4-1/4". $175-225.

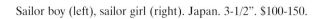

Sailor boy (left), sailor girl (right). Japan. 3-1/2". $100-150.

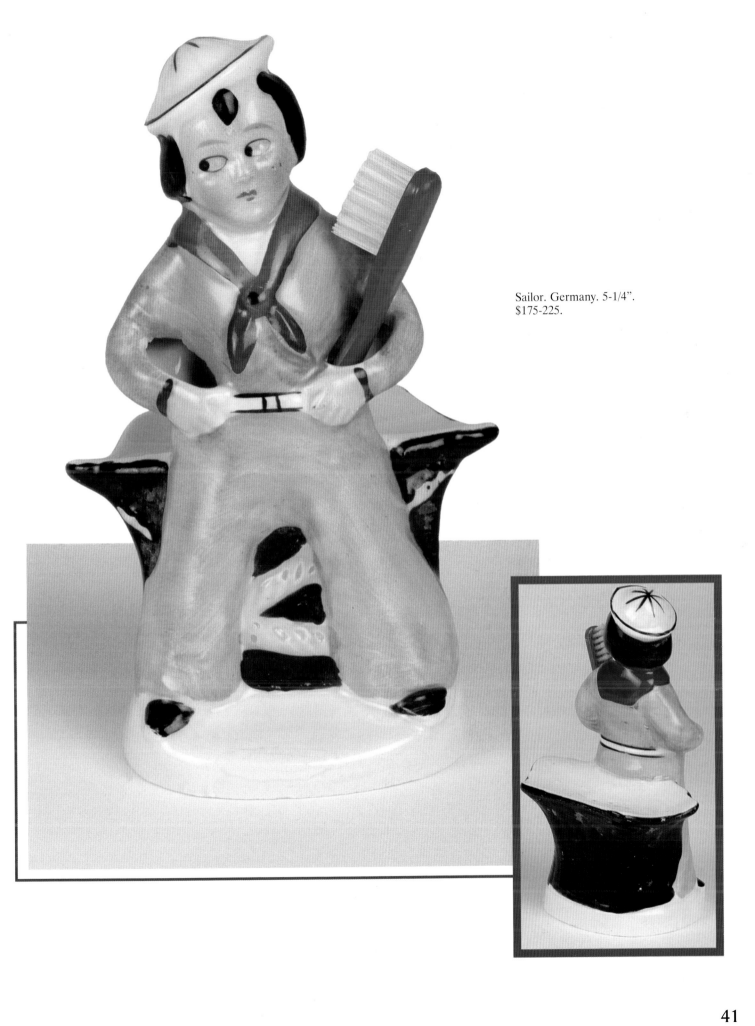

Sailor. Germany. 5-1/4".
$175-225.

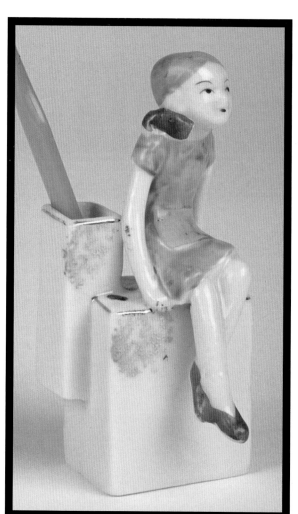

Girl in dress.
Germany. 4-1/4".
$250-295.

Girl sitting on wall. Japan. 3-5/8". $150-225.

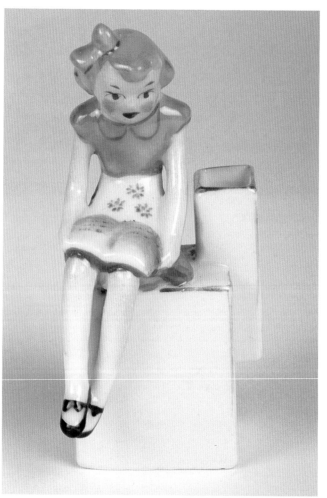

Girl sitting on wall
reading book.
Occupied Japan.
3-3/4". $125-175.

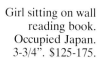

42

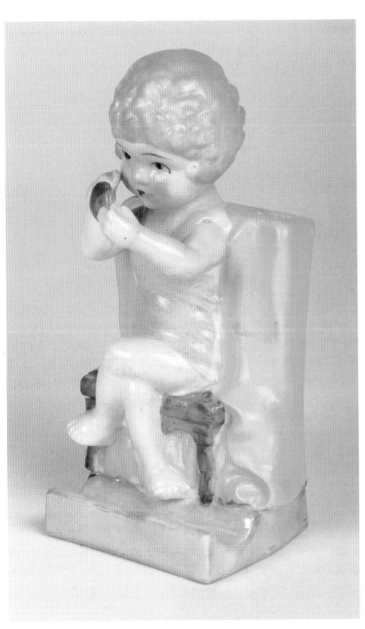

Girl powdering nose. "Copyright G.P. Corp.,"
Japan. 6-1/4". $350-450.

Girl powdering nose, bisque. "Copyright G.P. Corp.,"
Japan. 5-1/8". $275-350.

Colonial lady. Germany.
4". $250-295.

Girl brushing teeth. Japan. 5-1/2". $150-195.

Girl with bonnet. Germany. 4". $175-225.

Girl with puzzled look,
lustreware. Germany.
4-1/2". $175-225.

44

Girl with hand in pocket, lustreware. Germany. 4-1/4". $175-225.

Girl resting on right elbow, lustreware. Germany. 4-1/8". $175-225.

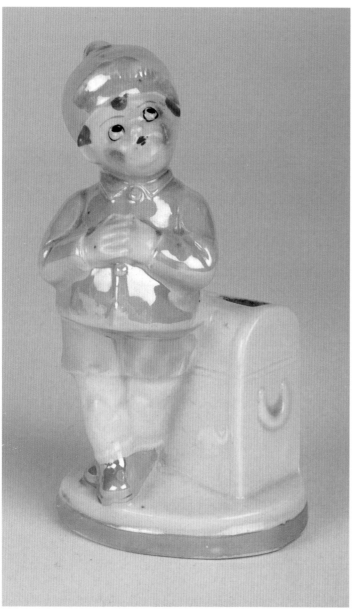

Girl with legs crossed, lustreware. Germany. 4-1/4". $175-225.

Girl sitting holding vase. Germany. 2-7/8". $125-175.

Girl reading book, Hummel type.
Japan. 6-3/4". $125-175.

Flapper in blue. Germany. 5-1/4". $250-295.

Flapper sitting with stole. "Poets je tandén." Holland. 4-3/8", $250-295.

Flapper holding two baskets. Reads "Poets je tandén" on back. Holland. 4-1/2". $250-295.

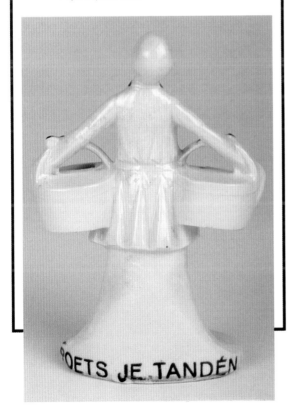

Flapper in slack outfit. Germany. 4-1/4". $250-295.

Flapper walking dog.
Germany. 5". $275-350.

Flapper in sleeveless top. Germany. 4-3/8". $250-295.

Flapper holding flower sitting
on lustreware conch shell.
Germany. 4-1/4". $275-350.

Girl with hands in pockets.
Germany. 4-1/4". $250-295.

Girl with dog. Japan. 5-5/8". $150-195.

Girl in rose. Germany.
5-3/4". $275-350.

Girl holding toothbrush and toothpaste, tray in back. In cold paint. 4-5/8". $175-225.

Girl in bonnet holding puppy. Japan. 5-1/4". $195-250.

Girl by stump. Lustreware, Japan. 4-3/8". $125-175.

Deco girl in hat. Japan.
4". $125-175.

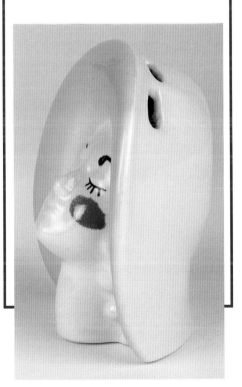

Girl in dress, bisque. Tooth powder holder.
Germany. 6-3/4". $350-450.

Girl in jacket, bisque.
Tooth powder holder.
Japan. 7-1/4".
 $350-450.

Girl in dress, bisque.
Tooth powder holder.
"A Price Product."
Germany. 7-1/8".
$350-450.

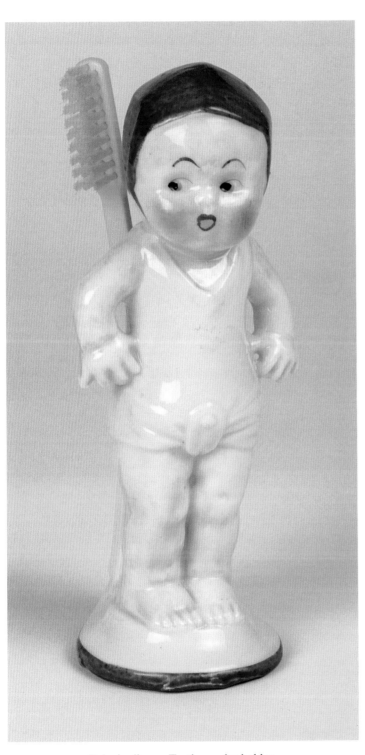

Baby in diaper. Tooth powder holder.
Japan. 7". $350-450.

Girl standing with muff. Tooth powder holder.
Germany. 6-3/8". $175-225.

Girl holding doll. Japan. 5-5/8". $150-195.

Corner toothbrush holder with girl brushing dog's teeth, lustreware. Japan. 5". $125-175.

Spanish girl. "Made in England." 3-7/8". $150-195.

Girl holding chicken, celluloid. Japan. 4-1/2". $250-295.

Scarved lady. Germany. 4-1/2". $150-195.

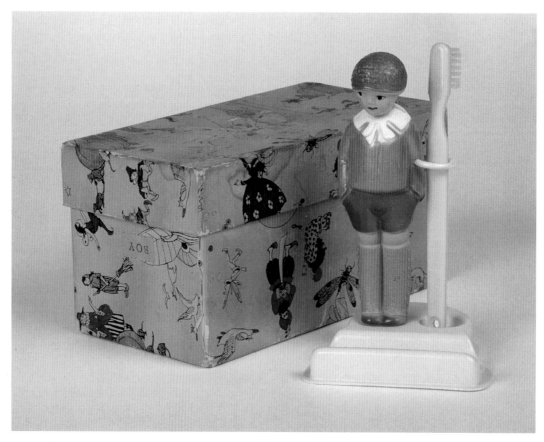

Boy, celluloid with original box. Japan. 4-7/8". $250-295, figure; $75-100, box.

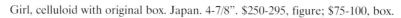

Girl, celluloid with original box. Japan. 4-7/8". $250-295, figure; $75-100, box.

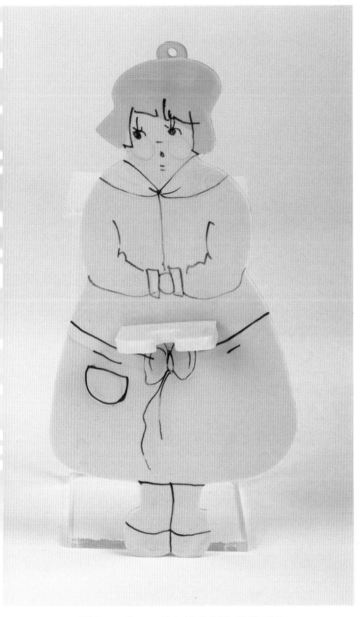

Girl standing, celluloid. 5-1/2". $150-195.

Witch. Germany. 4-1/2". $275-350.

Dutch boy with hands on hips. Japan. 5". $125-175.

Dutch girl. Japan. 5-3/8". $125-175.

Dutch girl. Japan. 4-5/8". $125-175.

Dutch girl holding cup and
spoon. Germany. 4". $250-295.

Dutch girl with basket on
back. Germany. 5-1/8".
$150-195.

Dutch girl holding sailboats,
lustreware. Germany. 6". $175-225.

Dutch girl. Germany. 4-1/4". $150-195.

Dutch girl by basket. "Rarukon Ware," Japan. 5". $150-195.

Dutch boy. Germany. 4-1/4". $150-195.

Dutch boy, artist signed. Germany. 6-1/4". $225-250.

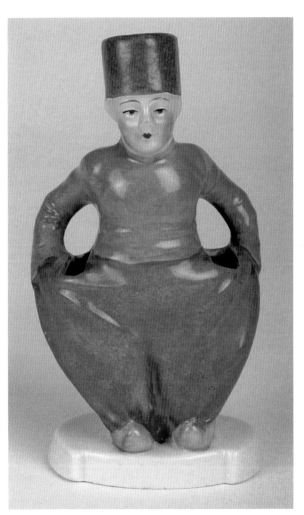

Dutch girl with hands folded. Germany. 5-7/8". $150-195.

Dutch girl. Germany. 4-1/2". $175-225.

Dutch girl with oversized pants. Japan. 4-3/4". $125-175.

Dutch boy with ladle, lustreware. Japan. 5-1/4". $125-175.

Dutch girl. "The Norwood Company, Cincinnati, Ohio, Germany." 5-3/4". Girl, $150-195; box, $75-100.

Dutch boy by tree. Lustreware,
Japan. 3-3/4". $100-150.

Dutch boy with basket on back. Japan. 5-3/8". $125-175.

Dutch girl with basket on back.
Japan. 5-3/8". $125-175.

Dutch boy and girl hugging.
Germany. 4-1/4". $125-175.

Dutch boy and girl sitting at European stove, lustreware.
Goldcastle, Japan. 4-1/8". $150-195.

Kissing Dutch boy and girl. Japan. 5-1/4". $125-175.

Left: Scotsman in kilt; right: Scottish lass. 3-3/4". $150-195 each.

Children in automobile, "Souvenir of Niagara Falls, Canada." Japan. 5-1/8". $150-195.

Sister washing brother's face. "Copyright G.B. Corp." Japan. 5-3/4". $195-250.

Swami. Goldcastle, Japan. 5-7/8". $150-195.

Swami with two urns. Germany. 4-1/8". $225-250.

Standing swami. Germany.
5-5/8". $250-295.

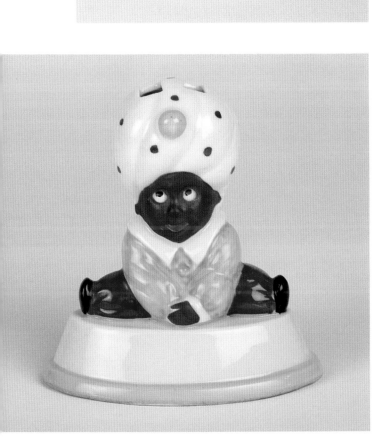

Swami sitting. Germany. 3-1/4". $175-225.

Swami sitting on base. Germany.
3-3/4". $250-295.

Swami with toothpaste box.
6". $250-295.

Swami. "The Norwood Company, Cincinnati, Ohio,
Germany." 6". $125-175.

Swami holding two urns. Germany.
4-3/4". $250-295.

Buddha. Germany. 4". $250-295.

Chinese man. Germany.
6-1/8" $250-295.

Chinese man. Germany. 6". $250-295.

Chinese man. Germany. 6". $225-250.

Chinese man sitting with legs crossed. Germany. 4-1/2". $250-295.

Bedouin with gun. Germany.
3-3/4". $175-225.

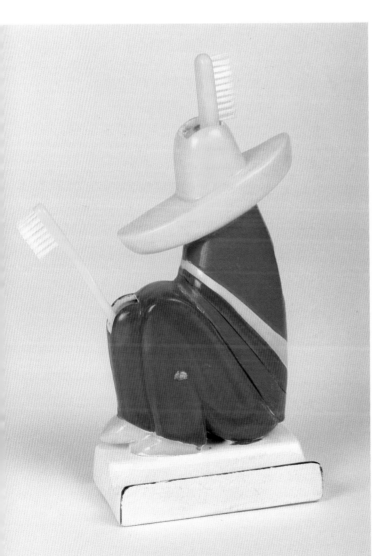

Black chef holding pineapple and bananas.
Japan. 4-3/4". $450-500.

Mexican at siesta. Japan.
5-7/8". $195-225.

Animals

Owl without tray. Germany.
3-7/8". $150-195.

Owl on tray. Germany. 3-7/8". $195-225.

Owl on base. D.R.G.M. (Germany). 4-3/4". $195-225.

Owl on base. Germany. 3". $150-195.

Owl by chimney. Germany. 2-5/8". $125-175.

Penguin in top hat.
Germany. 2-1/2". $175-225.

Quacker, with original box. "The Norwood Company, Cincinnati, Ohio, Germany." 5-5/8". Duck, $150-195; box, $75-100.

Songbird. Japan.
3-1/2". $195-225.

Deco crow. Germany. 4-1/2". $195-250.

Spotted songbird. Japan. 3-1/4". $150-195.

Walking chick. Germany. 2-1/8". $100-150.

Duck by drum. Germany. 3-1/2". $195-250.

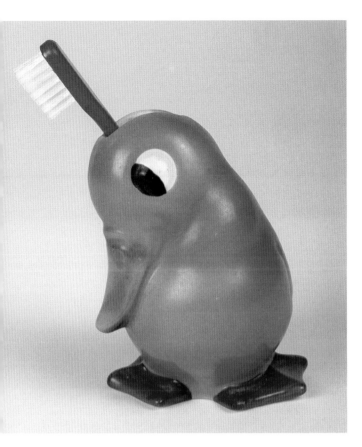

Duck with head turned.
Germany. 3-1/8". $150-195.

Whimsical pelican. Japan. 5-1/2". $150-195.

Duck on pedestal. Germany.
5-3/4". $195-250.

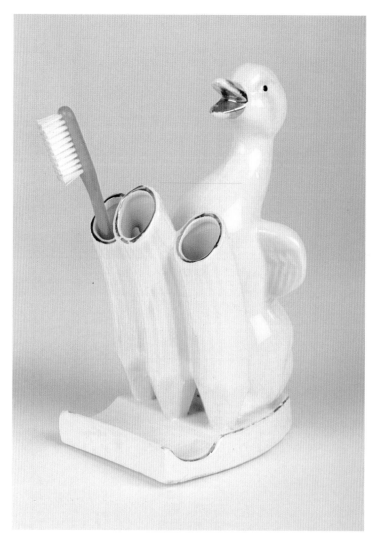

Duck with three reeds.
Goldcastle, Japan.
6". $75-125.

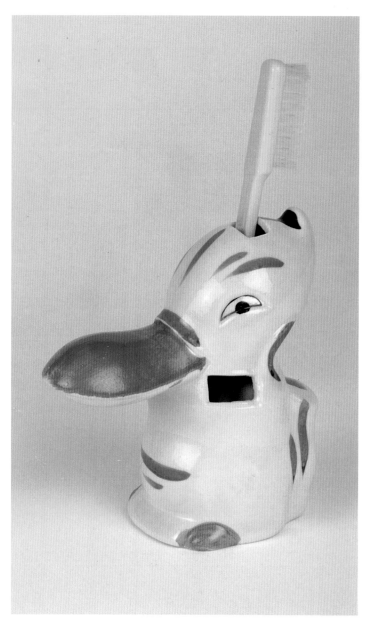

Whimsical pelican. Japan. 4". $125-175.

Duckling holding two
eggs with toothpaste box
in back. Japan. 5-1/2".
$125-175.

Toothbrush holder-towel set, celluloid. Duck holder, 4-1/8"; duck towel holder, 6-1/4" overall; chick holder, 4-1/8". $250-295 set.

Duck holding toothpaste, chalkware. "Copyright 1967 Miller Studio Inc." United States. 7-1/4". $100-150.

Deco cat. Germany. 3-1/2". $250-295.

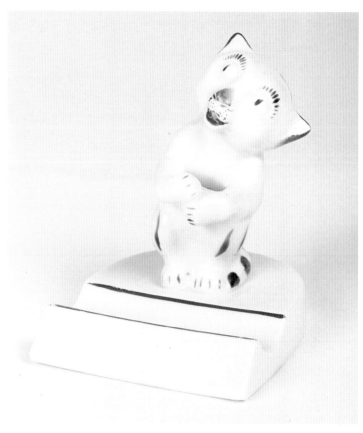

Sitting-up cat. D.R.G.M. (Germany). 3-3/4". $250-295.

...Cats

Surprised kitty. Germany.
4-1/8". $250-295.

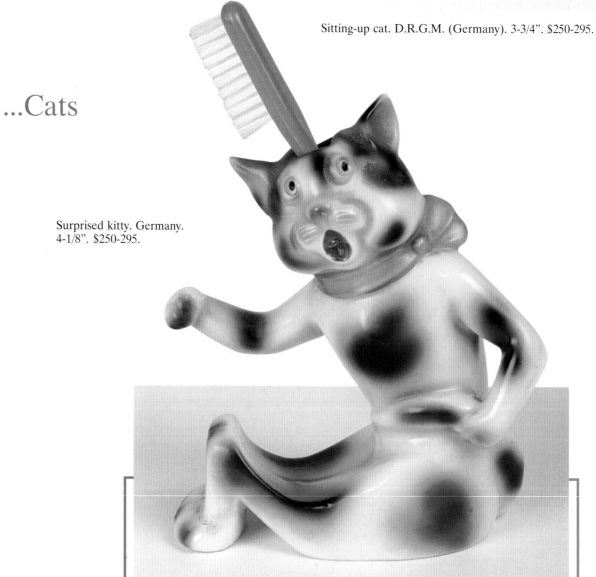

Kitten with bow. Germany.
3-1/2". $225-250.

Begging kitten. Germany. 2-3/4". $195-225.

Deco cat, sitting. Germany.
4". $195-225.

Spotted cat. Japan.
3-1/4". $150-195.

Halloween cat. Germany. 3-3/4", $225-250.

Cat playing fiddle. Germany.
4". $250-295.

Sitting-up cat. Goldcastle,
Japan. 5-3/4". $150-195.

Calico cat. Japan. 5-1/8". $125-175.

Sitting-up cat. Goldcastle,
Japan. 5-1/2". $150-195.

Hunchback cat, lustreware.
Japan. 3-1/4". $100-150.

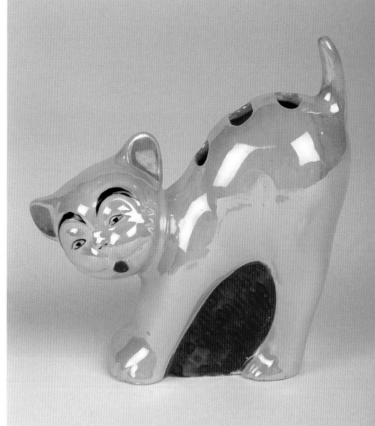

Sitting-up cat. Goldcastle, Japan. 5-1/2". $150-195.

Cat with haunches up, lustreware. Goldcastle, Japan. 4-1/4". $150-195.

Cat, with original box. . "The Norwood Company, Cincinnati, Ohio, Germany." 5-3/4". Cat, $150-195; box, $75-100.

Cat, chalkware. "Copyright 1957 Miller Studio Inc." United States. 5-1/2". $100-150.

TOOTH BRUSH HOLDER

This tooth brush holder will delight
The kiddies, it's so gay.
They'll want to use it every night
And several times a day!

Close-up of box.

Horse's head.
Occupied Japan.
3-1/2". $175-225.

...Horses & Donkeys

Steeple chase horse with
jockey, lustreware. Japan.
4-1/2". $195-225.

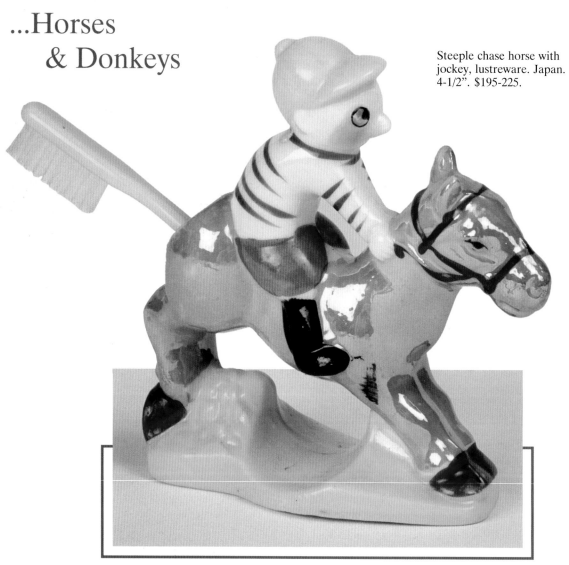

Steeple chase horse
with jockey. Germany.
4-3/4". $195-225.

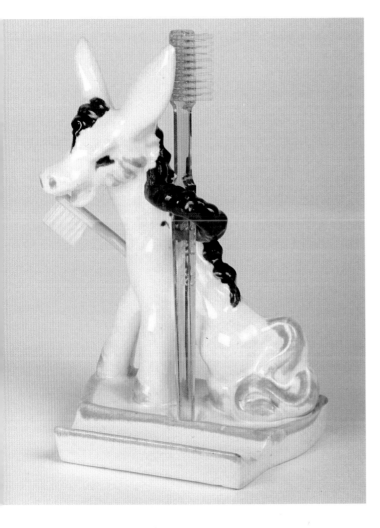

Trojan horse. Japan. 4-3/4". $195-225.

Sitting donkey. Japan.
5-5/8". $195-225.

Donkey with saddle blanket. Japan. 6-3/8". $150-195.

Sitting-up donkey. Goldcastle, Japan. 6-1/4". $150-195.

Rabbit with egg, corner
holder. 4-1/2". Germany.
$350-400.

...Rabbits

Flopped-ear bunny sitting.
Goebel, Germany. 3-3/8".
$175-225.

Flopped-ear rabbit. Goldcastle, Japan.
6-3/8". $250-295.

Walking rabbit with basket.
Germany. 5-1/8". $325-375.

Rabbit with broom and pail. Japan. 6-1/4". $250-295.

Sitting rabbit. Germany.
2-1/4". $150-195.

Rabbit with hat, "Brush and be bright." Japan. 4". $225-250.

Rabbit on base. Germany. 3-1/8" tall. $250-295.

Peter Rabbit (unsigned). Lustreware, Japan. 5". $150-225.

"Baby Bunting." Germany. 6-5/8". $350-450.

Celluloid rabbit with original Dr. West toothpaste and brush. United States. 4". $250-295.

Baby Bunting. Japan. 5-1/4". $250-295.

94

Dr. West Toothpaste figure box for
rabbit. 3-3/8" x 3-3/8" x 6-5/8".
$75-100, box only.

Rabbit, chalkware. "Brush your teeth." United States.
6-7/8". $75-125.

Rabbit with pipe and glasses, plastic.
6-1/4". $75-125.

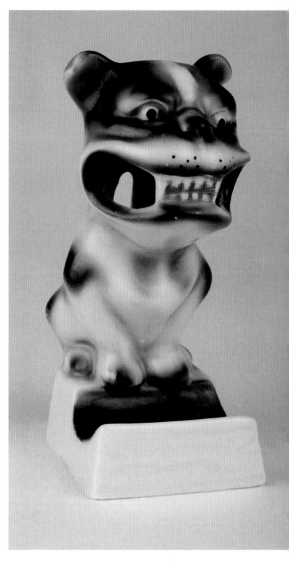

Growling bulldog. 4-1/4".
Germany. $150-200.

...Dogs

English bulldog with
oversized tongue. Japan.
3-3/8". $150-195.

Dog sitting holding two steins.
Japan. 4-3/8". $150-195.

Terrier with paws up. Goebel,
Germany. 4". $175-225.

Small sitting pup. Japan.
2-5/8". $150-195.

Sitting terrier. Goebel, Germany. 3-1/8". $175-225.

Small sitting pup. Japan.
2-5/8". $150-195.

English bulldog beside book.
Japan. 2-3/4". $150-175.

Puppy sitting by pot. Germany. 2-5/8". $150-195.

English bulldog with collar.
Germany. 2-5/8". $150-195.

Standing English bulldog.
Germany. 2-7/8". $250-295.

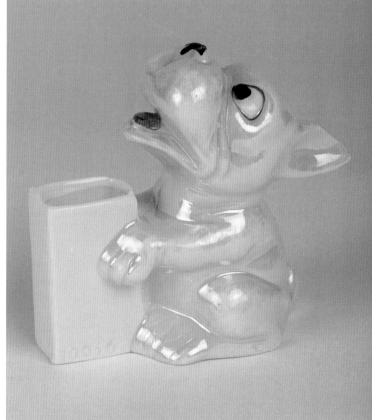

Happy puppy, lustreware. Germany. 2-3/4". $150-195.

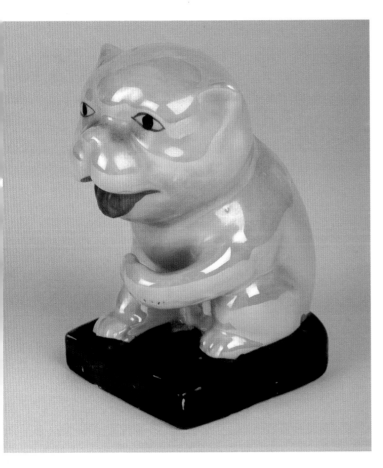

Puppy sitting, lustreware.
Japan. 3-1/4". $150-195.

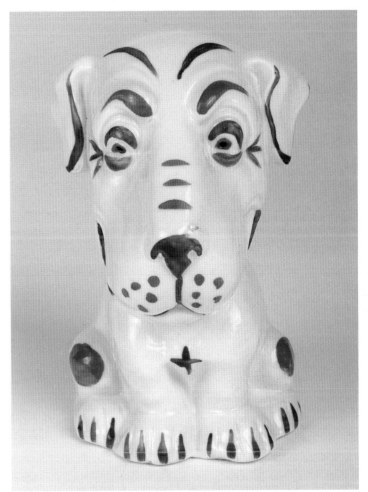

Whimsical dog sitting. Germany. 4". $125-175.

Sitting Dalmatian.
Germany. 3-3/4". $150-195.

Spotted pup. Japan.
3-7/8". $125-175.

Dog with tongue hanging out. Japan. 4-3/4". $150-195.

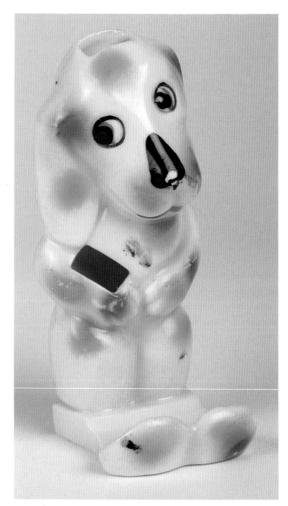

Sad spotted pup. Japan.
5-1/2". $75-125.

Puppy holding tray with soap dish. Japan. 4-1/2". $175-225.

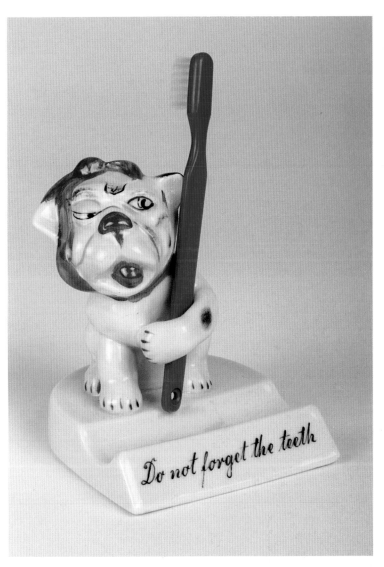

Dog with toothache, "Do not forgot the teeth."
Germany. 3-3/4". $250-295.

Deco dog. Germany.
3-1/4". $250-295.

Dismal Desmond. Germany.
3-3/4". $225-250.

Dismal Desmond, with box at back for toothbrush.
Germany. 3-1/8". $225-250.

Dismal Desmond. Germany.
4-1/2", $225-250.

Whimsical pup looking to left.
Germany. 3-3/4". $175-225.

Whimsical pup sitting. Germany. 3-3/8".
$175-225.

Two whimsical pups playing.
Germany. 3-3/4". $250-295.

English bulldog with one hole. Germany. 3-1/4". $250-295.

English bulldog with two holes. Germany. 3-1/4". $250-295.

Whimsical pup leaning back laughing. Germany. 4-3/8". $275-350.

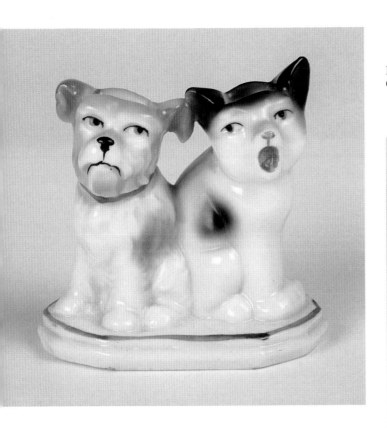

Best of friends, puppy and kitten.
Germany. 3-1/4". $225-250.

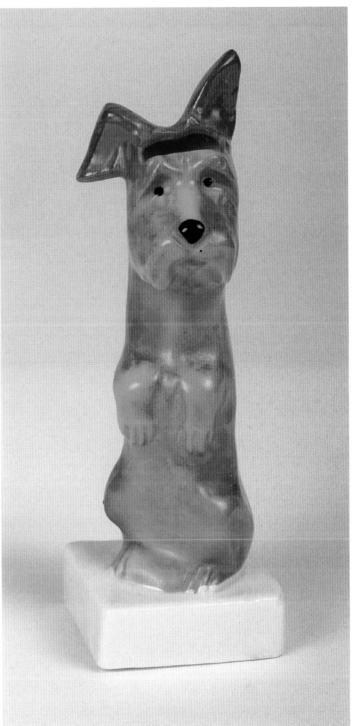

Begging Scottie. Germany. 4-1/2". $225-250.

Waving puppy. Japan. 3-1/2".
$175-195.

Two Scotties. Japan.
4-1/2". $150-195.

Scottie with two baskets and puppy. Japan. 6-1/8". $175-225.

Begging Scottie with basket. Goldcastle, Japan. 6". $175-225.

Corner toothbrush holders with twin Scotties, lustreware base and vase. Japan. 5". $125-175

Three Scotties playing cards. Goldcastle, Japan. 4". $125-175.

Begging Scottie, "Brush for Health."
Japan. 4-1/8". $175-225.

109

Whimsical terrier walking.
Japan. 3-3/4". $150-195.

Deco terrier.
Goebel, Germany.
4". $225-250.

Playful puppy. Japan. 2-3/8". $125-175.

Playful puppy, lustreware.
Japan. 2-5/8". $125-175.

Playful puppy. Japan. 2-1/2". $125-175.

Bulldog with haunches up.
Japan. 3-7/8". $150-195.

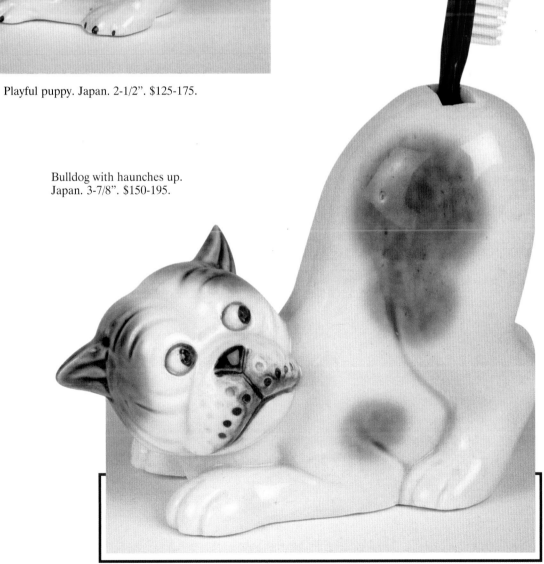

Laughing calico dog. Japan. 4". $125-175.

Sitting pup, "Spaghetti Face." Goldcastle, Japan. 4"$125-175.

Winking dog. Right: lustreware, Goldcastle, Japan; left: Goldcastle, Japan. 4-1/8". $100-150.

Sitting pup, "Spaghetti Face."
Goldcastle, Japan. 4". $125-175.

Puppy with mustache. Germany. 4". $125-175.

Whimsical dog sitting.
Germany. 4". $150-195.

Whimsical pup with swollen jaw. Germany. 4". $175-225.

Pup with paws to side. Germany. 3-3/4". $150-195.

Bulldog, "Souvenir of Canada." Germany. 3-5/8". $175-225.

Corner toothbrush holder with two
Afghans, lustreware base and vase.
Japan. 5". $125-175.

Puppy. Japan. 3-1/8". $75-125.

Laughing dog. Goebel,
Germany. 6". $175-225.

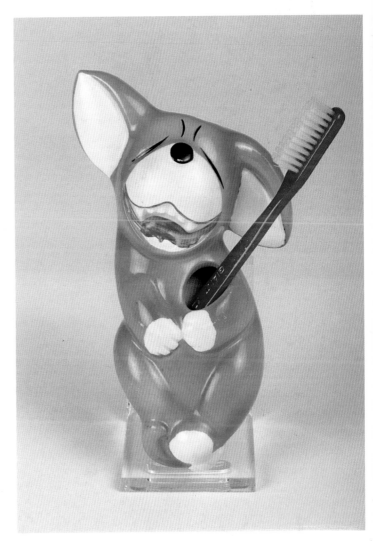

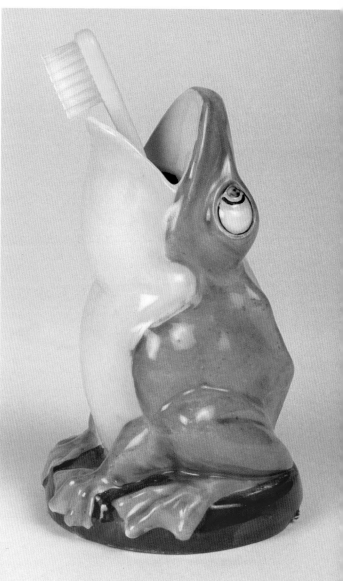

Croaking frog. Germany. 4-1/4". $250-295.

Sitting frog. Germany.
4-1/4". $250-295.

Frog with pipe. Germany.
2-3/4". $175-225.

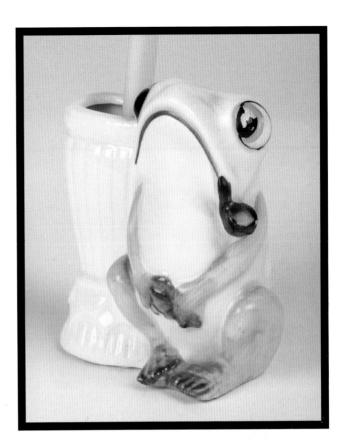

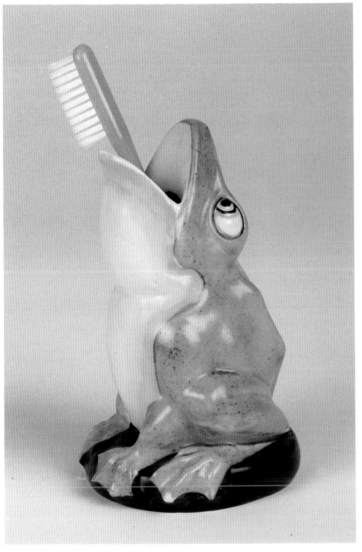

Frog, sitting up. Germany. 4-1/4". $250-295.

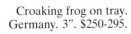

Croaking frog on tray.
Germany. 3". $250-295.

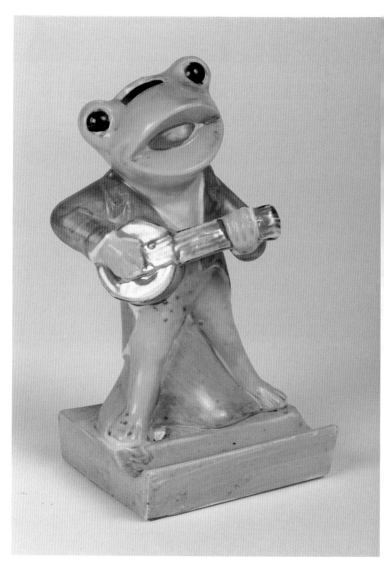

Frog playing banjo. Japan. 6". $225-250.

Frog playing lustreware banjo. Goldcastle, Japan. 6". $225-250.

Seated pig, lustreware.
Japan. 2-3/4". $100-150.

...Other Animals

Squirrel eating nut. Germany. 1-7/8". $150-195.

Pig dressed as chef.
Japan. 5-5/8". $195-225.

119

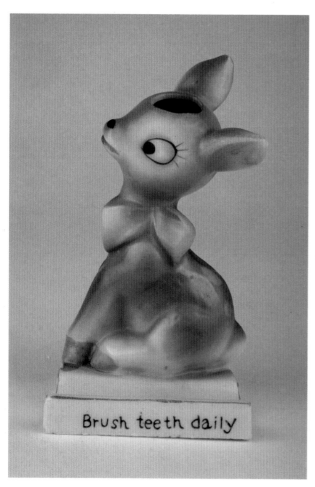

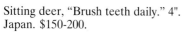

Sitting deer, "Brush teeth daily." 4".
Japan. $150-200.

Bear in jacket. Left: Goldcastle, Japan; right:
Japan. 5-1/2". $150-225.

Sitting polar bears. Left marked "Made in Germany;" right marked with crown. 3-5/8". $175-225 each.

120

Happy bear doing splits. Germany.
3-1/8". $150-195.

Sitting dressed bear. Japan. 5-3/4". $195-250.

Sitting-up bear. Germany.
4". $175-225.

Bear. "The Norwood Company, Cincinnati, Ohio, Germany." 5-3/4". $150-195.

Standing bear with head turned. Japan. 6". $195-250.

Standing bear with original label, "Bear in mind." Japan. 7". $150-195.

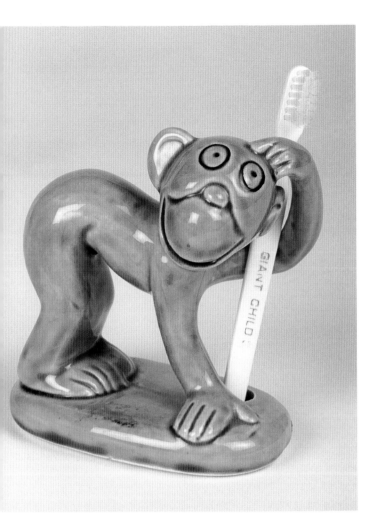

Monkey thinking.
Japan. 4". $175-225.

Monkey seated. Germany. 3-5/8". $250-295.

Monkey playing drum.
Japan. 3". $150-195.

Monkey seated with backpack. Germany. 3-7/8". $250-295.

Monkey seated with collar. Germany. 3-7/8". $175-225.

Sitting monkey. Germany. 3-1/2". $250-295.

Giraffe with tray. Japan. 5-3/4". $195-225.

Giraffe. Kane Enterprise. 6-1/4". $100-150.

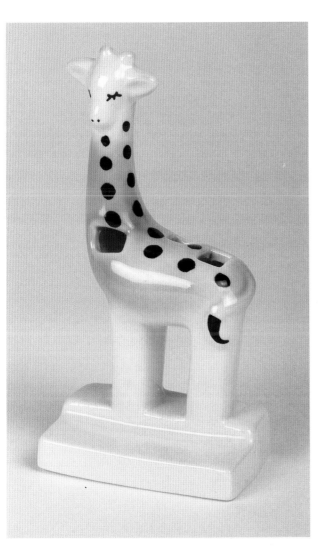

Giraffe without tray. Japan. 5-3/4". $195-225.

Yellow lion. Japan.
5-5/8". $150-195.

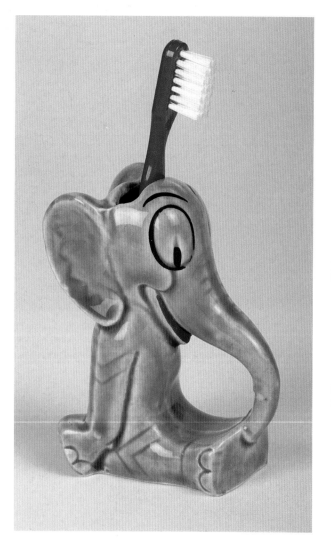

Sitting elephant with head turned. Germany. 3-1/4". $195-225.

Sitting elephant. Germany.
3-1/4". $195-225.

126

Elephant with howdah. D.R.G.M. (Germany). 3-1/4". $225-250.

Elephant seated, lustreware. Japan. 5-3/8". $150-195.

Dressed elephant. Germany. 3-3/4". $225-250.

Pink elephant seated.
Japan. 5". $150-195.

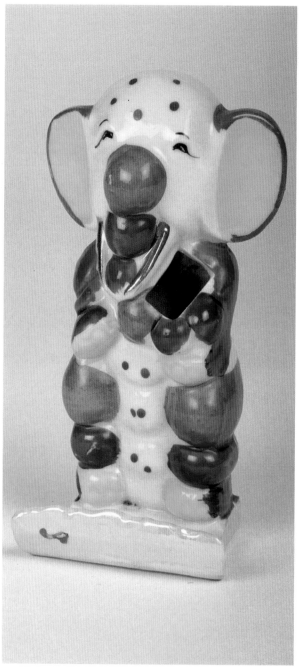

Elephant clown. Japan. 4-1/2". $150-195.

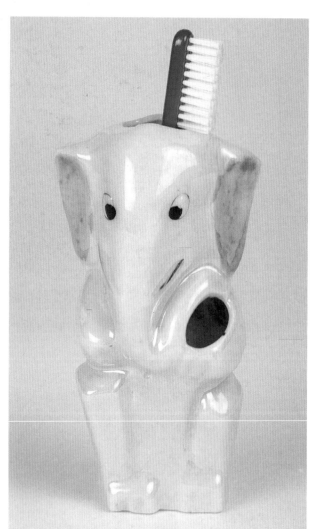

Sitting-up elephant, lustreware.
Japan. 4-1/2". $150-195.

128

Miniature elephant.
Japan. 2". $150-195.

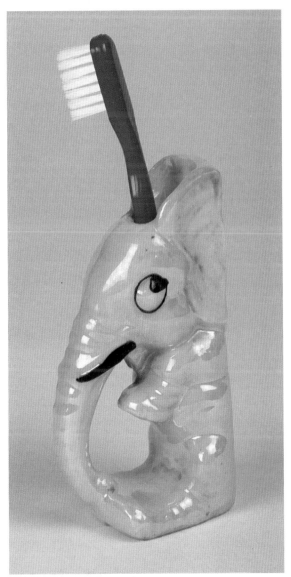

Seated hippo. Germany. 2-3/4". $225-250.

Sitting-up elephant, lustreware.
Japan. 3-1/2". $195-225.

129

Walrus. Germany.
3-1/4". $225-250.

Seal on drum. D.R.G.M. (Germany). 4-1/2". $225-250.

Seal on drum. Germany. 4-3/8". $250-295.

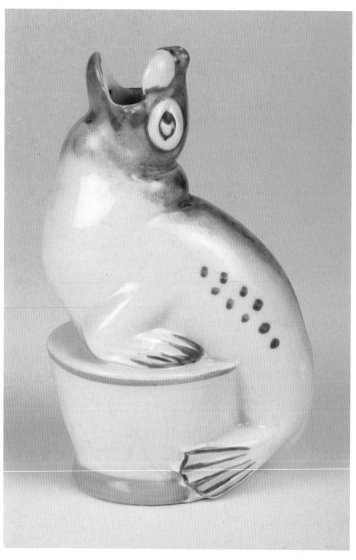

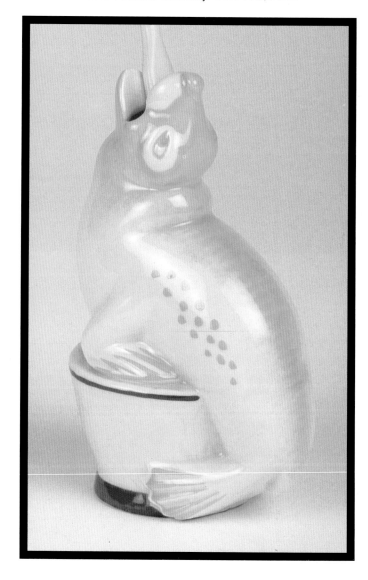

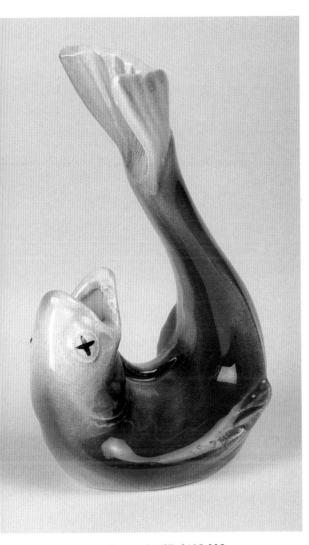

Fish, belly up. 4-1/2". $195-225.

Fish. 3". $125-175.

Cow. Japan.
3-1/8". $175-225.

Characters

...Disney

Pinnochio and Figaro, signed "Hand decorated Shafford." 5-1/8". $350-400.

Pinnochio. Walt Disney. 4". $1500-2000.

Gepetto. Germany.
3-1/2". $2000+.

Jiminy Cricket toothbrush set on original card, plastic.
"Copyright Walt Disney Productions." Dupont, United
States. Jiminy, 4-3/4". $150-195.

Jiminy Cricket. Maw of London,
"Copyright Walt Disney."
3-1/4". $1500+.

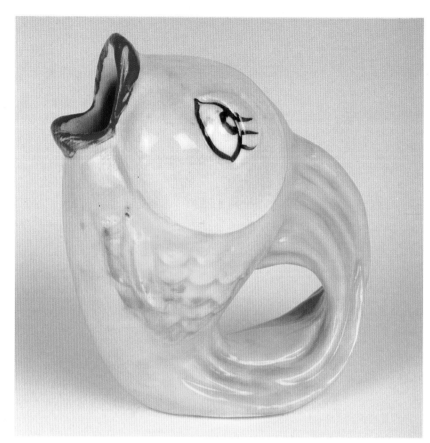

Cleo. Germany.
3". $2500+.

Tortoise. "Genuine Walt Disney Copyright, Foreign."
Germany? 4-1/8". $1500+.

Hare. "Genuine Walt Disney Copyright, Foreign."
Germany? 4-3/8". $3500+.

Donald Duck. Maw of London, "Walt Disney Copyright, Foreign." 4-1/4". $850+.

Donald Duck. Japan, made for Australian market, Copyright Walt Disney. 5-5/8". $1250+.

Donald Duck with head turned back. Left: porcelain; right: bisque. Japan. 4-5/8". Left: $1200+; right: $1000+.

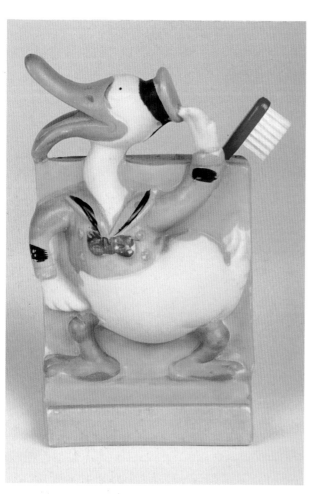

Donald Duck, "Copyright Walt E. Disney."
Bisque, Japan. 5-1/8" tall. $600+.

Donald with Mickey and Minnie. Copyright Walt Disney.
Japan. 4-1/4". $850+.

Twin Donalds.
Copyright Walt Disney.
Japan. 4-1/4". $850+.

136

Mickey and Minnie Mouse, bisque.
Copyright Walt E. Disney. Japan.
4-3/8". $850+.

Mickey Mouse, lustreware. Japan, made for Australian
market. 5-1/4". $1200+.

Mickey Mouse. "Genuine Walt
Disney Copyright Foreign."
4". $1000+.

Mickey Mouse Club toothbrushes on card. $50-75.

Mickey wiping Pluto's nose, bisque. Japan.
"Copyright Walt E. Disney." 4-3/8". $850+.

Pluto. Maw of London. 3-3/4". $1200+.

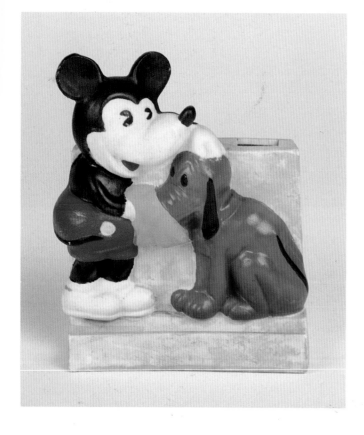

Pluto. Japan. 4-5/8". $1000+.

Doc, Sleepy, Sneezy, Snow White, Bashful,
Happy, Grumpy, Dopey. England,
"Genuine Disney Copyright Foreign."
Snow White, 6" T., Dwarfs, 4".
$2000+ set.

"'Doc' says brush your teeth.
'Snow White.'" "Walt Disney
Productions." 4-1/2". $125-175.

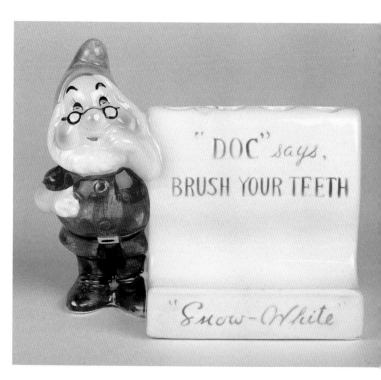

Snow White with dwarf. Japan. 4-5/8". $750+.

"'Doc' says brush your teeth.
'Snow White.'" "Walt Disney
Productions." 4-1/8". $125-175.

Sneezy. 2-1/2". $125-175.

"Happy," bisque. "Copyright Walt Disney." Japan. 3". $175-225.

Bashful. 2-1/2". $125-175.

Flower the skunk.
Japan. 4". $150-195.

Dumbo, bisque. "Copyright Walt Disney Productions." 3-5/8". $350-450.

"Three Little Pigs," bisque.
"Copyright Walt Disney."
Japan. 4". $250-395.

Three Pigs, bisque. Japan. 3-3/8". $275-350.

Three Pigs. 3-3/4". $275-350.

Pig playing fiddle. "Genuine Walt Disney Copyright Foreign." 4". $250-295.

Pig playing flute. "Genuine Walt Disney Copyright Foreign." 4". $250-295.

Frog band.
Germany. 3-1/4".
$2500+.

...Cartoon,
Comic &
Nursery
Rhyme

Flip the Frog. 3-1/8". $1500+.

Bonzo with side tray, on lustreware base. Japan. 3-3/4". $295-350.

Bonzo-type beside columns. German lustreware. 3". $175-225.

Bonzo laughing on lustreware base. Japan. 4". $295-350.

Bonzo playing horn, lustreware.
Germany. 3-1/4". $250-295.

Bonzo with head tilted, lustreware. Japan. 3-1/8". $225-250.

Bonzo holding tray. Germany.
4-1/4". $250-295.

Garfield. Modern. 3-3/4". $75-125.

"The Three Bears." Japan. 5". $150-195.

"Peter Rabbit." Japan. 5-1/8". $150-195.

"Old King Cole." Japan. 5-1/4". $150-195.

"Old Mother Hubbard." Tooth powder holder. Germany. 6-1/4", $350-450.

"Little Red Riding Hood."
Japan. 5-1/8". $150-195.

Little Red Riding Hood,
artist signed. Germany.
4-3/8". $350+.

Little Red Riding Hood, lustreware
hanger. Japan. 3-1/2". $125-175.

Little Red Riding Hood with wolf.
Germany. 4-1/4". $250-295.

Peter, Peter, Pumpkin Eater. Japan. 5". $125-175.

Old Woman in Shoe. Japan.
4-7/8". $125-175.

"The Baker." Goldcastle, Japan. 5-1/2". $100-175.

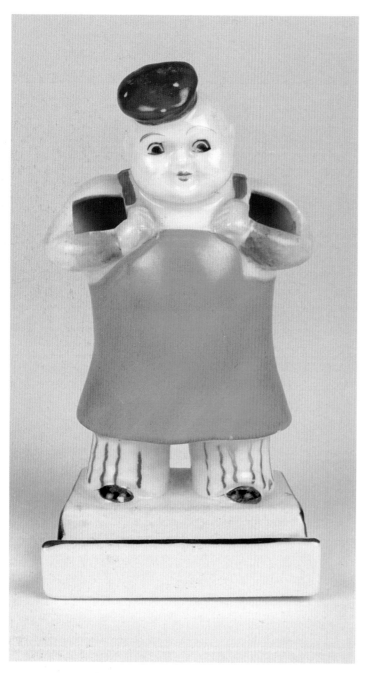

The Butcher. Japan. 5-1/4". $100-175.

"The Candlestick Maker." Japan. 5". $100-$175.

"Dick Whitington." Superior, Japan. 4-3/4". $225-250.

"Jack and the Beanstalk," lustreware. Japan. 4-3/4". $250-295.

Three bears. Imperial China, Japan. 4". $175-225.

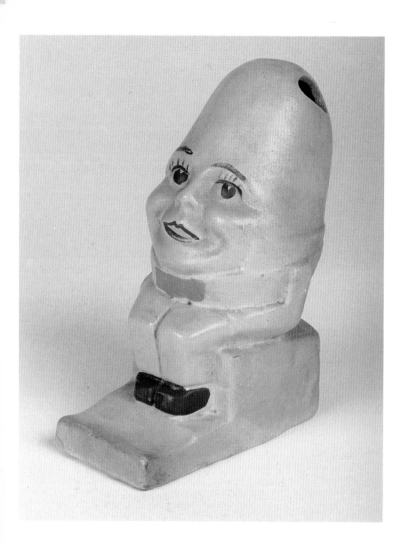

Humpty Dumpty, bisque. Japan,
"Pat. Pending." 5-1/4". $175-225.

"Orphan Annie."
Copyright F.A.S.
Japan. 5-1/8".
$325-375.

Little Orphan Annie and Sandy, bisque.
Copyright Famous Artists Syndicate,
Japan. 3-5/8". $250-295.

154

Uncle Willie and Emmy, bisque.
Copyright F.A.S., Japan.
3-3/4". $250-295.

Andy Gump and Min, bisque. Copyright F.A.S.,
Japan. 4". $250-295.

Henry and Henrietta, bisque.
"Copyright 1934 Carl Anderson."
Japan. 4-3/4". $600+.

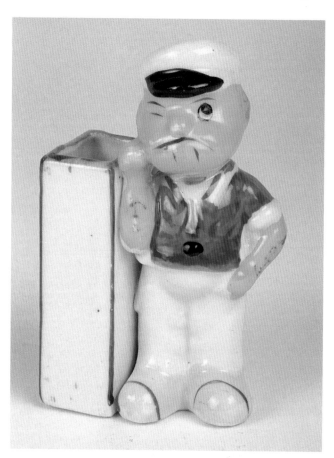

Popeye. Japan.
3-1/2". $150-195.

"Harold Teen." Copyright F.A.S. Japan. 5". $350-450.

"Ducky Dandy," bisque. Japan.
4-1/4". $275-350.

"Moon Mullins." Copyright
F.A.S. Japan. 5-1/8". $325-375.

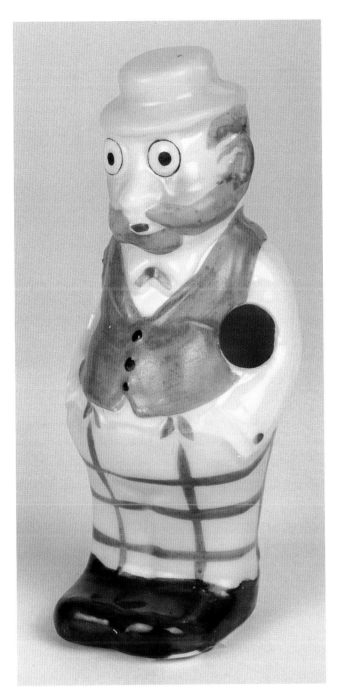

"Uncle Willie." Copyright F.A.S. Japan. 5-1/8". $325-375.

"Uncle Walt." Copyright F.A.S.
Japan. 5-1/8". $325-375.

"Little Tommy Tucker,"
celluloid. 4-5/8". $150-195.

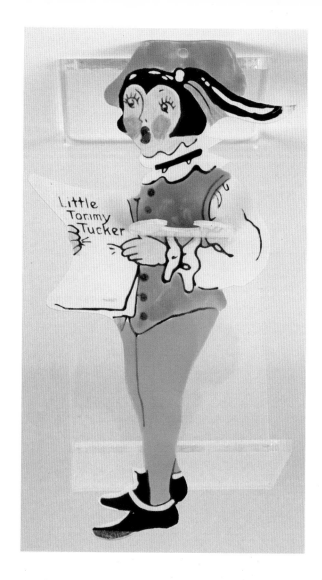

"Kayo." Copyright F.A.S. Japan. 5". $325-375.

Santa at chimney.
3-3/4". $100-150.

...Mabel Lucie Attwell

Empty pockets, signed by the artist Mabel Lucie Attwell. "Foreign." 4-1/8". $1250+.

Golfer signed by the artist, Mabel Lucie Attwell. Germany. 4-1/8". $1250+.

The Twins, signed by the artist Mabel Lucie Attwell. "Foreign." 4-1/8". $1250+.

Twins shown with a postcard with a postmark 1938.